NATURE OF THE HEART

NATURE
of
THE HEART
Poems for Holistic Healing

JACK ADAM WEBER, L.AC.

20 07

EARTHBOUND PRESS
PAHOA, HAWAII

EARTHBOUND PRESS
P.O. BOX 2130
PAHOA, HI 96778
808.938.2405

Grateful acknowledgment to:
Joseph Bruchac for "The Remedies," first published in *Entering Onondaga*,
Cold Mountain Press, 1978, reprinted with permission of the author.

Five Element Calligraphy: Yu Hong Chen

Winter Image: Judith Secco, www.judithsecco.com

"Xin" Calligraphy: Bob Schmitt, www.laughingwatersstudio.com

Cover Design: Jack A. Weber & Benjamin Cziller
Typography: Jack A. Weber & Stephanie Reedy

Library of Congress Control Number 2006907004

ISBN 978-0-9765248-0-9

Categories: 1. Poetry 2. Personal Growth 3. Holistic Healing
4. Self-actualization (Psychology)

1st printing: February 2007

Dedicated to my father, Robert James Weber,
for showing me the way into nature and words.
And to Charlene Johnson, for showing me
what to put words to.

THE REMEDIES

Half on the Earth, half in the heart,
the remedies for all the things
which grieve us wait for those who know
the words to use to find them.

Penobscot people used to make
a medicine from Mayapple
and South American people knew
the quinine cure for malaria
a thousand years ago.

But it is not just in the roots,
the stems, the leaves,
the thousand flowers
that healing lies.
Half of it lives within the words
the healer speaks.

And when the final time has come
for one to leave this Earth
there are no cures,
for Death is only
part of Life, not a disease.

Half on the Earth, half in the heart,
the remedies for all our pains
wait for the songs of healing.

— Joseph Bruchac

CONTENTS

火   I. *Summer*

土   II. *Indian Summer*

III. *Autumn*

IV. *Winter*

V. *Spring*

VI. *Silence*

Appendix

"Soulwork...involves breaking open the husks of the conditioned identities that encase our seed potentials...so that these seeds can blossom and bear fruit."

— John Welwood

ʬ 1NTRODUCTION
Breaking Open

Eight years ago I sat down to write an Introduction to *Nature of the Heart*. Little did I know that I would continue writing the piece for the next seven years. The result of that running off-page is my first prose book, *Healing Between the Lines*, due out in the near future.

The majority of the poems in *Nature of the Heart* were written between 1994 and 1998, when I was twenty-six to thirty years old. They chronicle the unbidden, full-hearted life that was broken open through body-centered psychotherapy and catalyzed by illness, holistic medicine, poem-making, relationships, break-ups, sacred psychedelic forays, and deep ecology. In hindsight, I see that the foundation for this opening had been set previously from years of yoga practice, meditation, and tai chi ch'uan, as well as epiphanies while gardening and living outdoors in the woods.

These mind-body practices and experiences provided the tools for feeling my way into the blocked—tensed, knotted, numb, unrequited, longing—areas of my body and its eventual freedom from backlogged pain. When not dealt with, past hurts become disenfranchised aspects of ourselves, inhibiting our ability to live from a deep place and give the best of ourselves. They form what I call "encrustations" around the heart. Our deeper, unacknowledged pains block our passion, sense of purpose and meaning, sensitivity, capacity to love and be loved, and many other whole-hearted qualities. These historical wounds prevent us from being truly present and fully alive in the moment.

One rite of passage into adulthood is to reconcile the wounds that keep us stuck in childhood patterns of reactivity and closure. Allowing our hearts to break open to re-live and release these seemingly stuck emotions preserved in the body-mind frees us up to discover hidden gifts locked inside of us. We can choose to see these petrified places in us as blessings in disguise. I remember distinctly the day that I developed a whole new appreciation for chronic, physically manifested emotional pain. That provident moment showed me how my body's intelligence had preserved the story of past trauma for later discovery and healing, when it was possible to read, re-live and release it. My pain served as a guide and gauge to undo the constraint, eventually revealing my true self that had squirmed around for years beneath the cobwebs and mortared walls of defensiveness. I was sunlight emerging from behind clearing clouds. The rays are poems.

Week after week, I began my psychotherapy sessions by sitting quietly, slowly scanning, sensing my body, feeling into its blocks, then releasing its story and trauma in whatever ways were appropriate in the moment: speaking, crying, wailing, stretching, or simply listening and observing. The means was not so important; *feeling* all of it was. Outside the therapy room, I would engage the same process for therapeutic writing, translating my deep heart's uncanny truths onto paper.

The figurative death and rebirth of my heart reflected—and quite frankly, illuminated—the natural metaphors of Taoism and Chinese medicine I was concurrently studying at Yo San University.

This mirroring of my soul's unfolding with the paradigms of holistic medicine is a primary reason for grouping the poems in this book according to the seasons. The seasons are the metaphorical, holistic framework of Chinese medical theory (discussed further in the Preface). Ultimately, however, it was core therapy work that unlocked and informed these poems from the recesses of my being, a place where I am paradoxically most and least myself—one with nature and its elemental forces, perhaps.

Most of the poems in *Nature of the Heart* are tools I used to reconcile my own heart encrustations, helping drop me into the seat of my soul. Others of these poems merely look out from this place of homecoming. Even the more personal pieces communicate archetypal qualities—human struggles and glories mirrored in natural metaphors common to us all. Over the years, people from many walks of life have shared with me how they benefited from the poems in one way or another. This has led me to appreciate further what Emerson once said, "To believe what is true for you in your private heart is true for all men: that is genius."

Below I include the original Introduction to *Nature of the Heart*, written in 1998. It is now the Preface to the poems. The five color pieces of calligraphy Poetry-Art at the back of the book are reproductions of my hand-made originals. These images also comprise part of my "Healing Poetry-Art" greeting card line.

I am grateful for this day, for the long-awaited serving of *Nature of the Heart* from the forges of time and the siphoning of the gods to make into other books. This collection, perhaps more than others now in the works, remains most dear to me. It records the beginning of a transformational period after which my life would never be the same again—not even close.

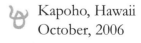 Kapoho, Hawaii
October, 2006

ʊ *P*REFACE
Poetry as Wholeness

While each of the poems in *Nature of the Heart* is complete on its own, I wanted to present them within a dynamic framework reflecting the whole of life. To this end, the poems are arranged according to the cycle of the Five Elements, also known as the "Five Phases."

As the metaphorical model central to Taoism and traditional Chinese medicine (TCM), the Five Phases represent the basic constituents of creation, the essential "building blocks" of nature. More importantly, the Five Phases also represent the cycles of transformation common to all life, a quality most significant to poetic healing and human growth.

The Five Phases are *Fire, Earth, Metal, Water,* and *Wood.* According to Chinese medical theory, each of the Phases corresponds with a different season of the yearly cycle: *Fire* with summer, *Earth* with late summer, *Metal* with autumn, *Water* with winter, and *Wood* with spring. Each of the Five Phases also corresponds with a specific internal organ, emotion, "spirit," color, climate, sound, health and disease pattern, and other attributes.

These attributes are called the *correspondences* of that Phase. The correspondences, as well as the transformational beauty of the Phases, are further outlined in the Appendix.

The correspondences of the Five Phases encompass all facets of body, mind, and spirit. The Five Phases, then, are a fluid and flexible poetic window through which the whole of life can be interpreted and creatively experienced. They are dynamic constellations of interrelated qualities that transform into and support one another in the endless cycle of birth through life to death into rebirth. Their unique holistic "personalities" of body, mind, and spirit reflect the interface and interaction of human nature with the natural world. Chinese medicine understands the macroscopic seasons of nature to be embodied in the microcosm of every human being. For all these reasons, the Five Phases make Chinese medicine holistic in the deepest sense.

Experiencing each poem within the season whose correspondences it most closely represents provides a holistic "treatment," complementing the ways that acupuncture, Qi Gong, herbs, and other methods of holistic medicine help us to integrate our holistic natures. Through this kind of poetry, we can more directly join the universal life energy upon which holistic medicine was founded. A basic understanding of holistic medical theory lends insight to the poems, as an appreciation of the poems increases our understanding of holistic healing. The last section of poems does not represent a specific season, but that from which all seasons arise, and to which they return.

Xin: ancient Chinese character for "heart" representing openness, elegance, strength, and flexibility. The heart is considered the "Monarch" of all the other organs; therefore, the heart embraces all the seasons.

~ I ~

Summer

火

Nobody has ever measured, not even poets,
how much the heart can hold.

— Zelda Fitzgerald

WHOLLY

The Heart
Truly Broken
Is Healed

Only Once
And Just
As It Is

Over
And Over
Again

*Written over three years, one stanza per year, this koan-like
poem stumps the mind—a perfect way to enter the Heart.*

CATCH FIRE

Walking out to sea
The body alive in purple waters
Reflecting red and orange sunrise.

What you do and live must catch
Fire to the waking depths inside you.
Do not settle for the concept of experience,
Writing what you will not lead
Or the burden of reading
What you will not be.

Following the birds to the horizon,
I lost this song
To fly.

HUMMINGBIRD

In the dark
Sea of your eyes
A hundred tears
Are shed
For the nectar
To remain
In your work
With flowers
Where you take
Just enough
To fire your heart
And speed your wings
To give the fruit
Of simple joy.

With soft lament,
You so tortured
So innocent
Your feathers once bright
Now sullied
In fervent discontent
Of me
And my friends
With minds
To twist and take
More
Than the tree's gift
Of flower,

Of nectar,
Of oceans
For love to live
Content.

Dear friend,
Please don't leave
Our world
Rests
In the well
Of your eyes
And the blur
Of your wings
In a moment,
Gone.

WILDFLOWER

Love has taken
My lover's hand
And run away
Back behind
My heart
Of withered dreams
And tethered tries
To some forgotten field
Of wildflowers and wildgrasses
Who barely hide
Their quick'ning ground
Of saving hands
To reach enclosed
The last of squalor
In my bones
And drink through me
The dark'ning sky's
Sweet water
Sacrament.

SARA

You, Artist!
Do not hold your light up
To dim love any longer,
To a father who never knew
And inside will never know
Your soul.
You paint with his blood
Your own canvas now.

The bridge and the river await you—
They know your name, Sara.
You did not remember them
To forget who you are!

Yet it *is* a struggle
To reach the bridge,
To clear the psychology
That burdens the way.
But the water will quench your thirst
And keep you
Drinking more
Without your having to leave
Or search very far.
For Heaven's sake,
It's all around you!
And returns the energy
Of the journey
Ten times over

To your aching bones
And withered skin.

Your beauty stands on its own.
But you refuse to see that
Or the bridge
Or the river
Or the mangled path
You must clear
And walk
To be found
By your eddy home.

Then you will swim
Not in the sea of onlookers
But from within their eyes
To see you whole,
Returned to the current
Where all the energy spent
Paddling upstream
To some forgotten ground
Does not have to be
The instinct of the salmon
Who struggles
Only to die
And lay its eggs.

We humans collaborate with calling
And birth it;
We die *to* lay our eggs.
But we are the egg,
The river
And the longing
At once—
Downstream,
Upstream,
The same stream,
We go where it goes,
It flows as we grow,
No logs broken beneath our feet,
No life vests to hold,
Only trust to be held
And receive
The beauty
We give.

SWEATER FROM MACHU PICCHU

The handmade sweater
My father gave me
Doesn't quite fit
As neatly as I'd like.
So I wear it,
As the most beautiful badge
My heart could carry
To keep me warm
After all these years
That truly twisted me
As the sweater does
Just barely enough
To remind me
Of ruins
And the love
That remains.

I MUST WRITE

And want to drown
In the words that keep me alive,
Birthed to the images they hold
For life held tight, coiled in aching desire
Waiting to burst forth and color the air
The wonder it knows
When we let ourselves flood
With the permission of love—

And die to this world,
To live inside its beauty
Cascading through the music of my flesh—
There alone with words and careful eye
To tell of what heaven forms the heart
With the permission that poetry gives.

My own response to Rilke's asking the young poet, Mr. Kappus, to question himself, "must I write?" If so, says Rilke, "then build your life in accordance with this necessity; your whole life…"

DESIRE

My heart a wild beast
Run away from me,
Caring not for marriage
And finite things
The mind can grasp,
Or for cautions
Of obliteration
It cannot see.

Only to behold
The awesome wonder
Of this subtle world,
At once flesh and sacred
And devour it untouched
In one grateful bite.

Its beautiful woman
Of endless desire
Disappears in a universe
Of unspeakable light,
Unmasking and coloring
Just another ray
Of sky and sunset:
Every inch of skin,
Every glowing feature,
Radiant now translucent
Opening vistas
To teeming forests

And fragrant meadows,
At once the vibrant spray
Of peacock's feathers
And endless horizon
In purpled waters
Resounding, trembling
In the song of ages.

Yes, this is the awesome and careless
Wonder of my love.
Indeed these reins of thought
Too short to contain
The free-ranging savage
Inside my chest,
For this sleek and ravenous creature
Of wholesome desire.

THIS GLORY NOW

Love arrived—
After the storm
Nothing left
But words of dust and ruin
Perfectly arranged
To scatter the ground.

Now pick them up
To light this cavern—
Hang them from your window
As a beacon
For the world to see.
You deserve their beauty,
This glory now.

I could be poor
Live in a small village
And write songs of love.

Instead, I live in a big city
Write songs of love
And am richer for it.

~ II ~

Indian Summer

Lay me beneath a yawning sky on a windswept shore.
Let me begin again, for I have faith in the land
and in the songs of my soul.

— Paige Deponte

SACRED

My feet welcomed the sand
And lungs the cool ocean air,
For it is nighttime
When the world can better find me
Alone by the sea
Letting my pores relax
From the onslaught of city vibe.

We meet again in this strange world,
Where the people must come to rest,
Where the sand and stars and waves of air
Meet the water lapping at my feet, smiling,
Saying, "I know, I know, you love me
A little more," because I care a little more
About the styrofoam and the plastic,
The car fumes and the garbage
That choke us
And the waters we call life
Dictated by some government folk
Who can't see beyond the gates
Of their own estate, more like a prison
For tomorrow's sunrise, it trickles down
To this small moment of space,
As I touch you water and sand
To feel you air and stars
In my chest, sad

That we and our children are already dying
And I can't change it

And I don't know what to do
Because it's so big
This race to die that we have lost
The joy to live,
Not the numbing of entertainment
Addicted to distraction,
But the raw life of joy
Moved to tears
Sprung from waters clear
And fertile land
That once grew each other strong,
We are weak and getting older
In our search for youth and constant pleasure
Clouding the source of life, unadorned
Right by the side of grief and sorrow
That must have root and place to grow
Amongst us creatures and the land
So we would change
What makes us sick.

A garden of rue in every home
So love could grow
Where fear had thieved
And distanced truth—
To pay the price
For consumers' waste
And live with trash
At our doorstep
Not off behind some hill

We never met,
Whose belly we never touched,
Whose hair we did not fondle
Light between our praying hands,

That the depth of life *could* renew
So death might be a wholesome parting
Returning spirit pure in shining flesh
To a soil rich with honor
Because we cared
To listen
And wisen our bones
To hear the quiet song of stones
Who remember the sacred way
To walk in beauty,
Not just for our children's sake
But for our own
As the only sane path to walk
For our children's children who
Play and laugh and roll
Upon the fragrant earth
Already in our hearts
If we are quiet enough inside
To hear
The centuries whisper
Through the pine needles
And the rocks bleed with tears
We never knew until we cared
To listen,

Until we learned
To be
The winter of our pain
So summer could truly return
To our hearts
Made full by breaking,
When we know
The barren sorrow of the valleys,
The land raped of trees
And the ocean's well of tears
Held back by pollution.

We must stop to feel
The true strength of what it takes
To be righteous,
To be old
In the face of nature
Before it's too late
For today to save us
From the addiction
To stay afloat,
A fake
Teetering above the dying Earth
On a heap of fear and waste
That robs us
From our true home
In the sun.

NATURE OF THE HEART

What were the body and the body of the Earth
But a bright'ning sky and painted ground,
And an open heart such art well lived
With thoughts homeward but trails of dust
Our bones entrust. For the kindest nature there persists
Of all the wild and wingéd things,
A meadow's blossoms bosomed high on fragranced clouds
And billowed air, a breath our flesh does breathe in turn.

For what inward gaze would not behold
Such torrents from above washed through
A rushing river's thought ensued,
On waves and rays so bright as thine, O song,
From hallowed bends the body's blood-remembering
Legend sends, words anew this pulsing drum to sing
And pretend a moment's life were born again.

Here the nature of the heart does whole
All worlds that can't be told
Nor in fancy fashioned stanzas scrolled,
Save with rhythm and in rhyme
A heart with heaven finds.

For what were its body but imagined soil,
And what were its soul but that encoiled?
What were its joys but fleeting fires on the wind
And its sorrows but in sea and sky once drowned?—
Tokens from ago now ripe,
A silenced tongue now pressed to speak.

O, this form does wish to yell a pure spirit's well
For what behind this rigid mask could tell
A lovely dove's wingéd lifting bells—

MEDICINE MAN

Born of mud, rising to the sun—
Bark and stone
The deepest beauty curls my blood
Resounds like thunder, deafening time.

Grunting savage of earth and beast
Slowly wading the thick forest mist,
Incarnating a language centuries past—
Breath so green, dark and laden
Mist and sweat develop my scent.

Before me, within me, maps and layers
Evolving, turning, weaving a wisdom
I cannot say.
Skin of layers, darkened soil
Breasts like memory I hold within
Peeled from time, dissolved to soul, flesh and love.

Millennia tinged a verdant spark, pulse a landscape
Inside I see the world before me—
Gathering roots, smelling leaves
This is home eternity says,
Never a choice from heaven unknown.

I hold my heart so you may see it
Let go, let go
A depth inside I cannot say.

SAN JOSÉ CREEK

Stones,
Nay I speak before I know
That I am you and soon become
The clear and rushing by your side,
But from the voice the stars broke out
From where they could not
Longer live so closed in tight.

Now inside me wince a million sparkles sing
To see the rain and lightning thunder scream
Laying down the softest touch,
A tiny feather's raindrop ripple
Holding close the sandstone walls
To free the quickening creek
For wind who blows a stretch of time
By me crouched beneath this rock,
Clothed and naked to the setting sun
Nearing close the breath of night
Perilous wonder, lost to the rain.

CREATION PRAYER

O Sea,
O Sky
Drunk with tears
How happy I am
To see you blue
Still with rain
I cried
Once ago
To make you
So.

CAREERS

Careers are ruining the world.
Mine helping you
Heal symptoms of your career
And yours giving me
What I'm too tired to do
Because of my career.
All the while, life hovers
Eagerly to meet us
Beneath this great tapestry
Of career's selfish offerings
To preserve distance in flesh.

People may always fall ill
And waterlines become blocked
And what one loves to do
Surely be there to help.

But do we live this truthfully anymore?
Or not, to create
More careers and more noise
To avoid feeling
The great regret
At the gates of silence
If we stopped
To live
Wonderfully simple lives
Full of honor, respect and compassion
Upon the earth we insult

By dividing, raping and selling
For a career
Creating other careers
To buy
What isn't even ours
To spoil the fun
Of stopping
To breathe
A reverent life
Constantly squeezed out
Of the small cracks
In the sinews
Of our bodies
Where we have the choice
To stay,
To feel
Wonder
And give ourselves
To the call of beauty
We all sense inside
But are afraid to know
For fear that it may love
And ask of us
More than we know
How to return.
When this is how it is anyway—
That we belong to the great silence:
To the stars, to the rivers, to the trees.

We do not make careers out of life,
We are life's career.

Find not only what you love
But what loves you
And fills you
With a great sense of importance
To disappear in your place
Among all things
Instantly touching the heart
Of creation,
As I do tonight
Writing-being written
On the ever-emptying
Page of life,

Trembling and grateful.

I actually collapsed on the floor as these last lines came to me. I remember not even writing them, just realizing them, shaking and crying. My life changed with this poem.

EARTHOME
for Deborah

Listen,
The earth is your body,
Listening...
Rivers course your blood
The pulse of wave's breath
On the oceans.
Mountains house your soul
The sun your eyes to see.
Elder stones remember
The heritage in your bones
For breaths of wind
To move the heavens
And caress your hair
To grow the trees and meadows,
Their muscled legs turning down
Through darkened feet
Of tunneled soil, flourishing rich
To nourish your thighs, bending flesh there
The curve lines of hillside, all glimmering
In emerald pools of mind,
Clear and still...

Now dream, dream my quiet child,
And when you wake
From the rest of ages
Still on the ground,
Before your eyes
Can tell the light of day,

Know you are held
In her heartbeat
All through the night
That bathes you now
In a quiet vibrant stillness
Lingering in the dappled mist of morning
Above the land where you have slept away
The dream of thieves and lies.

LEAFBLOWER LIES

The leafblower lies,
Red trail of gasoline
Bottom of the river dead,
Killed by sanity's rage.

Said it would help us along
But dust, fumes and
The roar of bleak bareness
Left us
Blind in a world of heartless stakes,
Void of loam for a righteous rotting
To *truly* live, again.

Now upstairs
The birds return
To deafen us with tainted tunes,
And trees again keep their own
Close to home
Polluting the ground
That unbearable color
So close to fading, while

Behind the escarpment
White trash grows
Nervous and uneasy
Scared and queasy, for

The leafblower's dead
We said,
Sunk to the mire
Of deepest hell's fire.

THE CITY OF MY MOUNTAIN

Each day I bow before her,
If only inside myself.
Every day I let go
To her graces.
Each day she holds me
In her presence.
And sometimes I go out at night
To sit
In the dark by myself
With her good company,
Mystified glorious remembrance.

In this city you can be fined
For parking too long
On the dirt road
(Not long or fine enough)
Leading into that wilderness
Any day of the week.

But there is no law
That requires us
To visit the mountain
Even once a week,

Nor should there be.

ROSH HASHANA PRAYER

Dear G-d, of this tacit-torn Earth,
Of this "happy, healthy" *New* Year?—

Waiting for the stoplight
Your sad son looks up
From behind wrinkles
Of deep-etched sorrow
At the billboard,
Transfixed on its imaginary
Never-giving goddess,
Forsaking the last
Memory of forest and deer
That still breathe
Beneath the pavement, his Bronco
And all the other horrors
Layered over this land
To hide
A richer bounty,
And our souls
Still in the ground
Suffocating, screaming
For us to return.

*My Jewish upbringing taught me to omit the "o" so as not to write
the full name of G-d. I preserve the tradition in all my writing,
to stay close to my family, and to circles.*

~ III ~

Autumn

*Why would you try to reject any discomfort, any misery,
or sadness? After all, you don't know what these forces
are working inside you.*

— Rainer Maria Rilke

RETURN

The body too adjusts
To slanting light
As nature's vibrancy
Settles into muted anxiousness
Of winter coming.

Sunset branches hang
With leaves, quiet
Waiting for nightfall
And the growing depths
Of restoration
In coming months
When rain will quiet
The stupidity of the city
And follow the narrow
Undulating path
Deep into the reservoir
Of hope for all things.

Clouds darken thickening air,
A lone dove puffs its feathers
Shivering on the wire,
As the great sky engulfs
The last shadows of summer.

A deep sense
At the marrow of life
Remembers this shifting
Course of light

Across the heavens
And the chill of returning home
To the sap of remembrance
Where life's blood runs thin
Before the company of awareness
To fill it
With the substance
Of meat and meditation
In the stillness
That is autumn.

LEAVES
for Dad

Wavering unmoved in the faithful sky
The sentinels of my childhood home
Belonged to the trees and the wind
As much as I to the autumn of my youth
And their great return to a patient earth.

They were the unfound words,
The rattling reminders
Waiting to be written,
Released when ready
On the cradling breeze
In perfect and careless descent
To the empty page of the lawn below,
Soon to be collected
Onto the family tarp
Where I would play
Immersed intoxicated
By the full fresh flavor
Of leaves
That still remind me
Of everything that was good
About growing up
And all that could never be
Spoken at home.

There among ethers and aromas
I learned the immensity of life
And a blood-born friendship

I had with Ashes,
Towering beyond
My small-awed figure
To keep me company
While I searched the pattern,
Hidden voices
Among phrases of sky
Joined at once by an imperfect landscape
Of sand and soil, weeds and branches
Uniting the fragments of life
As the space and change
That spelled out the context and color
Of beauty and wonder.

Just beyond the well-kept lawn
The woods sprawled out
In all directions,
Where we walked
My father and I,
And found a different home
That lives inside us
Until this day.
Away from a life of tractor and rake
We distracted ourselves
With bird book and binoculars
Leaving vigil of the body
Between us

To the pungent loam
And flavor of the woods
A secret company of naked souls.

Alone together in nature,
The founding grace
Unknown to me then
That guides my heart now
Through my father's hand
As my own
To a future he could not write
He gave his time and patience
Teaching me how to read
The "rat-a-tat-tat, rum-a-tum-tum"
Of *The Little Drummer Boy*
Whispered into my ear
And how to follow a beat
In the silence of the woods
Its leaves tapped out for me.

*Written for Dad's 70th birthday, "Leaves" was originally
eight pages long, and a mess. It remains one of my most
extensively reworked poems, just like our relationship.*

ALCHEMY

Like vinegar of
Expectant grapes
The heart draws inward
To the quiet chambers
Of transformation
Waiting in darkness
For resurrection
By the thirst
Of its own juices
Spilled by life's sacred accident,
Aching
With a now growing.
Hopefulness
That comes with enduring
Grief's deliverance
From bitter days
Waiting to ripen
Elegantly sour
Painfully sweet
And wisely aged,
Strangely blessed
Ready again
To taste the world
Anew.

FALL

About to fall
Through a bed of thorns
To the rest of my soul
I am afraid
To die
To the lie
As a child I learned
To hide
A bigger life
For little love.
Now, I cannot
Live another day
Away, uncrowned.

STILL

Beyond the fog
I thought I felt
Your footsteps
Rumbling still
In the earth
Before me,
As I walked
Out to the night
By my mother's house
The sweet moisture
In the air
Wet my lips
For the first time
As I knew it was ·
You I had met
Out by the stables,
When the ground
Was still soft
From the storm
And the way
You touched her
With your feet
Six months ago
To ease the tension
Between us that day.

The Sapote tree took me
By surprise,
The way the fog

Makes things new
Before the eyes
Wandering through it,
Its fruit still falling
Turning the earth
A sour pungent sweetness
As I walked up the hill
With the memory of you
Still in my feet and chest
Wondering how all the old things
In this body are still carried
Into the thick, rich night

By the Sapote,
Whose fruit I felt still green
On the branch
Filling themselves each day
With the jubilant shouts
Of schoolchildren
In the fragrant mountain air
And occasional sunlight
To remind us
Of what heaven breathes
Through the present passing moments
Of how I miss you,
Still.

UNDONE

We all must pay
To be undone,
This alone is true.
Sweet wine
Pouring from our chests
Percolating down
The intricate collapsing
Labyrinth of bony pegs
To forgotten holes
(Who forgot themselves?),
Combustible writhing ecstasy,
Perforated sinews of G-d's
Seaming grace.

We give
Then give in
Return,
Of what we are not
For holding on,
Then of who we are
For letting go.

This is why,
Accept what is yours:
Where money has come
With peace of mind,
Or grief carved a hole
And left you undone,

A Red Sea parted
To firm the way.

We each must balance
The task of creation
To open—
Each gift comes with it
The challenge to return
What is left
Undone.

EXILE

There you wait, true emblem of life—
I
Distorted again, crawling back
On dry sacks of breath dragged over parched rocks
Exhausting the tired earth,
Return again from inflated misnomers deserted.
Everything now at once
Wheezing, squealing for you
River bath of water, breath I left for another,
Carry me, hold me, don't let me out
To my will again.

Hear the wind blow through hollows,
Here the winds blow from beleaguered flesh,
Here the deluge rises to meet the empty clouds,
Here the sun lives throwing words like wishes
To the howling air—I'll write my way back
Home I say, Home I will,
Returning tradewinds' bellows.

*Burned out, giving all my energy to striving for perfection in
Chinese medical school. My will pushing and pushing to get
good grades, a demon I fought with and celebrated. Not sur-
prisingly, I graduated Valedictorian, a very tired one.*

The Delicate Feather of Choice

Everything beneath it had changed.
Mountains were moved,
Boulders in my belly
Tossed aside
And tons of earth
Shifted behind my eyes.

This huge decision
Now needing just the wind
To fall my way
And blow these thoughts
Homeward.

The delicate feather
Of choice
Now resting
On a bed
Of firm delight.

*Are you willing to be sponged out, erased, canceled,
made nothing? If not, you will never really change.*

— D.H. Lawrence

COLD

I stand before the Earth, cold.
Shadows rise from my reflection
In stolid blades of grass,
Dew stripped from their weathered stalks
Beneath a silent screaming November moon—
Silver, bright my chapped face
Reflected in its eerie brilliance
Melting tomorrow to one black river
Coursing an endless line
Back to the one still brilliant stone
I cannot feel or fathom a touch,
A sliver of its hidden light.

My own sinews cracked in the autumn night,
The slow distant pine needles rest in quiet misery
Against a darkened sky,
And in me wells the name of creation
Pooled longsight to the bitter end
Of all seasons that pass and return
In the endless struggle with grief.

Not a piece of me can touch
The landscape of pain
Hovering inside.
Motionless, unanswered, undefined,
Misted across this absent cemetery,
Ages of wisdom and shattered hearts
Coalesce like pageantry
Deep in the still black well

Of my winter soul.
Nothing can reach the love
Ripped from my breast and belly—
The longing, the bleak refusal of the void
To rescue my hope
From ever wanting, ever clinging, ever loving
Anything at all.

Nothing,
Nothing can touch me there,
But despair.

BENEATH UNDERNEATH

Beneath underneath
Walking on glass
See through to a place
We cannot know
Walking talking driving
On roads
That never speak
The word below
The spoken tongue
Here above
The land of shallow glances
And futile touch and go
Be merry live a life
That never arrives
At the foot
Or heart
Or fiery core
Of great mystery
Where I go tonight
Alone
To be answered
Alone
Beneath the world
Of pleasure be
The dark takes me in,
Whole and empty.

O Lord,
Where do you live
In my heart
A thousand lives
Have sinned
Not loving you
For the answer
That lay me down
At last to rest
When this tired road
Has seen no more,
Bereft and broken
For your balm
I cannot know
You on the other side
Of death and danger
Where we do part
My love and I—
Give me strength then
To die
Here for you now.

Oh, what brittle shapes
We make by day,
The invisible One
A secret promise
I long to know
Waits beyond the stumbling blocks,

The doors locked tight
To fear and sight.

Then give yourself to faith—
Pregnant experience
Of trepidation
Braided and born
To worlds unseen,
Awakened truth
To carry us home.

Whales: A Farewell Dream

If only we could see
What the eyes cannot
Our time holding on
To what had long ago left
Could be spent saying farewell
Dear friend, fragment of ourselves
That served us well
To reach this place of meeting
Something greater
That calls, wells and rises
From within the greatest
Unknown part of ourselves,
Found only by listening
To what needs to live
And noticing
What wants to leave,
As stepping stones,
We mistook
For final fluid truth,
Trodden upon
To bring us home.

Now high above a cobalt blue
Beyond the drop of cliff,
I watch the whales below,
Their huge strength
Glistening and mirrored backs
Swaying, moving, undulating

Rhythmically and effortlessly
Up and down
In the current of the sea.

And I know that power,
It has been calling me back
From this dream I could not live,
From my belly I could not feel,
The whole body now
Filling with their motion,
This beauty that rests
At the end of trying
To become what we are not,
Just the whales now
And the careless, careful
Unstoppable freedom
Of the sea,
Where it carries us,
How it asks us,
To trust in the invisible
Strength of form
And not
The form itself.

MOONFACE

I looked upon the ocean
And there in the glimmering wake
Saw her face and felt her beauty
Caress the water and all her wonder
Shining there in the winter's night.

And I knew then
That I would always love her
And find her everywhere.
For, to empty like this
I've swallowed oceans
And mine at last
As creation sings
What it can
Only with her.

To tell you what I know
Or how to be
I'll point to the sea and the heavens
And let the raging waters
Drown my breast in tomorrow
Carrying out their wildest tumult
In the midnight hours
When we are asleep
And no one can see.

SOLSTICE

I threw that feather to the wind
In hopes of something greater,
To belong to the silence
Calling us back
Through the cracks in the clouds
And pores of our soul,
To the age-old way
Of giving to gain
What could never be kept.

This day then we kiss the sky
With open arms,
Reaching out to lose our minds
Deep within the dark inside
Of some tidy ceremony
To remember an empty self
And the great migration of life
Blowing through the brittle branches
Of that sandy cliff where we all stood
Kept warm by the dampened grass
And the aching pulse of our blood
For a new dawn.

We gave back our hearts
To a beckoning sea
Crying desolation
To that impossible explosion
Of scarlet fingers

Across a brilliant water
Bending the horizon there
Behind our eyes at sunset
As we watched a whole day end,
A fire stand still,
To wander through the night.

Each Winter Solstice I give away something precious to me; this year it was a pheasant feather I had found in the woods.

DARKNESS

O darkness, who visits me softly
Cascading down the endless walls of my soul—
Where do you go O darkness,
Where do you take me?
So quiet inside
Like velvet flowing, rippling, ripping
Through the corners of my body,
Where would I be without you to hold
My meaning, my glory, my pain,
To contain the hidden knowledge
That keeps me so sane?
Tender hand creating space: rancor,
Rancor erupting in your wake—
Ethers, dust and ashes remain: windows
To worlds unseen, bleeding
Through the memories and years.
You are pain, you are hunger,
You are depth in my eyes
To a thousand worlds.
You are stillness,
The beautiful lingering stillness
Comforting the room tonight
With your sorrow, the yearning, the tomorrow,
Tears I've denied
Since beginning of time, the fears
Of humanity a million years that fill
The oceans, return to your belly
To quench your thirst and return our souls.

You, the dull warm comfort
In which I rest, touch me gently,
Allow the wound to bleed in your arms;
I give you my life, my pain, my soul.
I give you my child, my hope,
My ashes, my glory.
Quiet darkness caressing my cheek,
Easing through my skin, softening flesh,
How I give to you, how you hold me,
Bleed black through my veins, return me
To source.

I love you, darkness, as I lay here
To rot in your hands—
Let the Phoenix through, let it
Call out to the night. Let it hug
My remains close to its belly. Let it
Screech, sound out the birth
Of this man from hell, rubble and ruins.
Let it howl, scream my greatest desire
From this deadest space, in me it rises
Clean, unscathed, like a jewel, somehow
Darkness so clean in her work.
Alchemist, friend, transformer, taking
My hand, returns me to her brilliant womb
Undone, unknown, full of memory,
Reflection of earth, of glory, a warrior, gallant,
Soft, entire, broken, a glaring sparkle silently

Rings through its edges
The beauty of G-d.
Death, rebirth, return and surrender:
Life, light and darkness—my friend
My closest friend, perilous, resounding
Guide to love.

WATERBOAT

Why so many practices   to channel life?   Let Life practice
being itself with you!   What already exists   in the world
came long before   you began   to practice it.   But you
have made   yourself   an island   to its strength,   refused
its daily pleadings   and enticements   to join its currents
in your own particular way   of riding being carried   in that
sea   which ebbs and flows   of its own   inside   yourself.
This separation   has made you waves   to break   from the
great flow   that crash   and die now   at your own shoreline
of resistance.   There was only one wave   that rose   from
the beginning of time   as a ripple in your eye,   more like a
rising crest of hope   in the sea   of your longing. So, time
to jump in   to your boat   made of water itself   and learn to
trust   this sea   loves you already,   holds you and wants you
to be   all that it is. But your droplet   must get wet   with
its desire for you. Stop trembling   on your desert island
collecting and trying to protect   your belongings   from the
great storm of life   come to wash away   all that doesn't last
to make it easier,   to give you an opening   to join   its
awesome fury.   Let it fill your days   with beauty   instead
of your bucketing out   its nourishment   to the small
container of yourself   to fill the void   of your life.   This is
so much work!   Jump in my friend,   the water is warm
feels good   and bathes you   in freedom. Let go of "I" and
all you think   you are here for Love   requires surrender.
Give your life   to the ocean,   to the self   where there is
no filling   to be done.   You are filled   in that   one act
of giving   up. We were all meant to swim   and be swum

with, not collect water into leaky vessels of thought for fear
of not having enough   to swim in.   Your body is this current
of life force   waiting   to join the sea.   Find where the island
disappears   and you become   the immensity   of the world,
entered into its domain,   its memory,   its reality of the way
it all began   and has always been   when you were too busy
trying   to figure out   what to do   with it.

BUOYED

It is not
Because something on this stagnant surface
Didn't work out to find you home.
Rather, your life swept under
And all around you,
Lifting and carrying you
Up and away
To your true abode
In the buoyed current of the river,
Flowing fresh and crystal clear
To hold you
More 'suredly and givingly
Than any life raft ever could,
Because you are the water's
Fluid enveloping freedom
Supported on all sides
From within
Your particular destiny in the world.

You are not the fly
Repelling water
Feeding on the dead debris
Of fear
At the surface
Of a murky pond.

TONIGHT

Across a seamless sea
Of liquid meaning
Oblivion bubbles and slides
Before the mind entranced
Following the secret path
Opening at moments
Unnoticed unforeseen
Creation is born
Taken by surprise
The body and senses release
Beneath a fallen pattern
Of wave and shoreline
To follow the edge
Of drawing tide
Whose white effervescent
Ever-changing
Maze of shape and form
Reminds us
Not to indulge
In the finite design of nature
Nor follow blindly its narrow path
Whose secret promise is to find you
Face to face embarrassed always
With your boring self
In some small corner of the world
Too small for your heart's desire
To accept the silent invitation

Life offers at subtle moments
When the tide reveals
Its true form
In the surge of power
That whips the night air
In silver misted wavecrest shouts
From an invisible G-d
Who loves the mystery
Behind your eyes tonight
In the candlelight
By the glass
Before the window
Through the moonlight
That separates me
From your strength
Out on the ocean
In my veins
Aching to find you,
Forever.

Written on several napkins at Gladstone's restaurant in Los Angeles during a friend's graduation dinner. Bored to death by the guests, I found other company, for an overall great time.

Rest of Longing

Trust those places
        With no way out,
                The dark corridors
                        Of your longing.
In fact,
        Entrust them more
                Than you give to daylight
                        Which disappears with fall of night.

Only hidden light
        Who waits for you in shadows
                Can reveal the invisible passage
                From darkness
                        That leaves nothing
Behind.

Quarter moon

On the water
Follows me

As my soul
Finds me

Wherever I go

~ V ~

Spring

Problems exist for the sake of better solutions.

— Anonymous

THE DIVING BOARD

Watching,
    Slowly
        At first
            Walking,
                To running steps
                    Of exaltation
                        Waiting,

At the last moment
        Frozen,
            With anticipation
                Praying,

                    Before leaping,
                        Soaring

From what we know
    To what we love,

            From what we were
                Into who we are.

BIRTH OF A POEM

In quiet moments,
When the formless sea
Of unfound words
Shows its heart
To a steady hand
And patience allows
The mind to part,
Are pushed forth
The seeds and prints
Of what has been,
You will find
The gentle stream
Flowing untouched,
Trickling always
At the bedrock of your soul.

Find there drops of wisdom
Like fallen stars
To scatter the page
For the silence they hold.
This alone the mind cannot see:
The sweet return at the center of beauty,
The sweet return at the center of beauty.

We must be naked
In the midst of creation,
Undone by the utter failure
Of its tempting promise

To receive the silent faith
Of its brilliant waters
At the blessed shores
Of a waiting heart,

Like sunlit dust
In the empty space
Of this quiet room.

SPRING

A tiny trickle in the wood
Playing love to the sleepy grass
Must have heard us coming,
As we met giving life,
Each to the other.

For it could have run and we have walked
There all alone and never known
This thread of light
Moving through the edge of night
Come to greet us fresh with words
From hidden spring, saying,
"Winter has passed. Winter, has passed.
I love you now from blind seeds
Of winter faith in whom you swallowed
The only flower to live again,
And know me now."

As we turned and walked away,
Filled with the silent language
Of the brook, I remembered
What has loved me,
What has learned me,
What has taught me
How to live *the only life*
All these years and months.

PRAYER SEED

I release you down
Between encrusted thoughts
And rocky habits of aged terrain,
To find your way
Into the dark
Earth of my dreams
And sink your roots
Into the deep
Soft glow, water of truth
You find there
To drink in a vision
For us to grow
Up through the center
Of my body, gathering
All its cells into the clear
Green strength of your life
For us to open our leaves
To a future sky.

So disillusioned and ill after seven years in Los Angeles, I used to recite this poem before sleep in order to get back in touch with where and how I belonged. "Prayer Seed" sprouted my move to Hawaii.

PENNIES AND CHANGE

Keep your money
Laced with resentment
And choked with guilt.
Take back the pennies
That matter so much,
And when their weight
As a rock
Upon your chest
Has pressed your mind
To this source
Of grief undone,
Take the rest
To build for bars
The prison of fear
Already you are.

Only then
Might you see me
From your lonely tower
Dancing in the fields
With rags and tatters,
Both hands clasped
Before my chest.
But for now
It seems
I build these walls
That keep you caught
To your own disgrace,
I, your lover's body
No more.

Only when
The world throws back
The reins you offer
In disguise,
They being dumb and blind,
Will leave you to
The source
From which they climbed,
With them still
Wrapped around
Your neck and mind
Stumbling blind
In your corner, doing time.

Might then you see
These paths of pain unwind,
Your heart undone.
But this I could never plan,
For one who is blind
Cannot see
Even with healthy eyes,
As one who cannot give,
Cannot, even by offering.

For me then,
It is enough
That these pennies as chains
No longer weigh upon my days,
That I might love you

From afar
And pray in earnest
For flowers to bloom
From dry lagoons.

TODAY

When the weary pursuits
Of all the days
Have hardened the heart
And silenced love,
The body must break
To undo time
And live again.

For now, as it has been all day,
A gorgeous silence fills the air,
As I look out the window
To the sunlight
Hugging the space
Between the leaves
A golden yellow green
Drinks in the breath of heaven,
Unafraid.

If only we could love
So easily
In the name of beauty
As everything else revels
In the silent gift of nature,

As petals now
Unfold the harbors
Of my mind,
Seeing for the first time
The hidden chamber

All these years and ignorant paths
Have brought me—
That I allowed this brilliance
Through the trees,
Through the clutter and pain,
That peeled away
The husks of innocence today,

Exactly as it is.

*This was a blissful day, one of many during the era of emerg-
ing into the light (or better, as the light was finally emerging
from me) after years of intense emotional cleaning house.*

ODE TO THE JASMINE

You, soft petal of moonlight
Sweet phosphorescence of night,
Grow as your friends, other faces
Toward and by the sun.
But you have lingered, bathed there
With her Highness, Lady Darkness,
Absorbed that essence of nowhere
Everywhere into your delicate branching body
Now shed it, as Persephone herself
Unveiled through thick green stems reaching
Into pink purpled blossoms emptying
For lighter ways filling the silk white face
Of your knowing beauty, holding
Back the night of night, monsters
Behind the trembling, confident silver flutter
Of your pale complexion, its jewels
Emerging through pure perfumed presence
Now emanating drunk and drifting
Through cool air—
Budding sweet reflected essence,
Healing balm of patient light
To sooth our hearts and ease our minds
Of fragile things that haunt our days
Neither you nor I could wholly absolve
Without your magic
Transformation of night.

Rain

Tonight I opened the door
To the rain,
Come to soften my skin
And fill the city streets
Like a stranger
Not noticing
The distance between
Me and the water,
The cement and trees,
My soul and heaven,
Come to greet me,
To revive the space
And narrow the distance
Between what I know
And refuse to live.

REMEMBERING BIRTH

A new bud
Opening from centuries
Of unremembered calling
Reaches forth from roots
Of truth it can't yet hold.

The body writhes
A tortured mess,
A blessed garden,
Greening for the going home—
Contorted weaving past and present,
Toiled tilling for the germ,
Last year's crop fodder for
The journey new.

One life passing
Another emerging,
One Life holding
All the seasons
From the depths
Of everything
That brought me
Here.

GATEWAYS

Maybe there is nothing
Firm at all,
One gate unto another,
Each passage a decision
To change everything forever—
You, the world,
The gates themselves.
There is nowhere
To turn back
The person
Who began
No longer exists.

This life of make-believe tricks
Always emptying itself
To love—

Now at the threshold,
Do we step in
To lose or include
What allowed to step from?
Or must these worlds
Of separation always exist
For longing to make life
Just the hope of truly living?

~ VI ~
Silence

寂静

From silence, beauty. From noise, pollution.

— J.A.W.

EXCEPT IN THE LIGHT

There is no shelter
For honesty,
No protection
For a true soul
Wanting to speak
Its secrets
From the well of silence,
Save in what you had
To say to be saved.

Create a new home for yourself,
To live blatantly
With your chest open
To heaven and creation.
Drink freely,
Then prepare
To be battered,
Scoured
Of all you are not.

AND THE SOUL SPOKE

Never injured to begin with,
I have no interest
In being healed—

Just had to be
Cracked open in this
Beautifully painful way.

Not getting over things
Allows them to move us
Into broader spaces—

Leaving just a trace
In the wings
They opened.

REMINDER TO ONESELF

You poets,
People, all
Small creators
Of great things
Singing—
Use these words
To translate
Your arrival,
Then be cautious
Not to stumble
Upon your tongue,
For only silence
Will float you
In this world,
The aloneness
That loneliness
Has been trying
To teach you.

CENTER

Everything circles
'Round the center.
Find the center
That lives outside yourself
Circling 'round still
A larger center
That draws you near,
Moving the center
Inside you.

Everything is born
Of motion
'Round an empty silent stillness
Waiting to explode with color.
True centers love
Other centers
With no firm place,
No fixed plans
And nowhere to go.

THE POET

Drop
    Drop
        Drop
            Drop me

                Beneath the earth
                To a world of shadows,
                For I do not belong
                To this life
                Of pretty shapes
                And was born
                From some other night
                Of hidden light to shine.

                Have you seen me?
                I go under creation
                Ducking always
                This form of figment
                To reveal what lives
                Beneath the crust
                Of hardened hearts
                And deadened pleasures.

                There are few words for me,
                So I let silence and song
                Do the talking
                For what can't be known
                Between careless tongues
                And neglected ears.

Whatever your talent
Is a gift—
Hold it lightly
Before the Lord
That you may be of service
To silence
That must speak so loudly
To the world.

WORDS OF SONG

The words of song
Must ease the mind
And sooth the body
As effortlessly
As a mountain's edge
Meets the sea,
To relax the back
And soften the belly
In whom they rest,
Carefully translating
The valley and space
Between consonant and vowel,
Phrase and linebreak,
Where smooth ridge of meaning
Drops perilously supported
As rain and wavespray
In an act of courage
It can't escape.

We all can go there,
Finding
The sweet rhyme
Of our calling
In the world,
The peculiar satisfaction
Of reaching out
To create
What already exists
Inside before trying,

Before beginning,
The inward translation
To meet creation untamed
On its own terms,
For our own sake
To be found .
In bluff meeting sea,
As rock and water
Dissolved to sand
Carried to infinity's bottom
To rise again, awash
In the splay of dunes and beaches.

These lines then
As vast, as broad a way,
A passage and current
For the heart to enter
This cruel and beautiful world,
As majestic and scary
As the beginning
Of all ends
We reach for
In triumph
And in vain.

TOILET PAPER

A pretty journal

Will not write

Good poems.

But a tortured life

In the fiery hands of love

Will convert toilet paper

Into flying sheets

Of magic—

EPITAPH

To sleep
On the horizon
That star I
Lived already
Before this birth
To dreams

In memory of R.M. Rilke

Appendix

THE FIVE PHASES
and their correspondences

火 The FIRE Phase corresponds with SUMMER, the Heart and Small Intestine organ networks, the emotion of joy, the tongue and speech, compassion, desire, Heaven, the sun, flowering and fruiting (fruition), the blood vessels and circulatory system, a climate of heat, the South, the color red, the planet Mars, the bitter flavor, the corn grain, and the sound of laughter. The "spirit" of the Heart is "Shen:" the faculty of mind, intellect, and our embodiment of universal spirit.

During summer, Fire's exuberant energy is gradually transformed into the nourishment of Earth, symbolized by Fire's ashes being composted into soil.

土 The EARTH Phase corresponds with INDIAN (LATE) SUMMER, the Spleen-Pancreas and Stomach organ networks, the emotion of worry, pensiveness, self-reflection, the mouth and sense of taste, food, nourishment, Mother Earth, nature, centeredness, groundedness, abundance, creation, the flesh and muscles, the digestive system, a climate of dampness, the Middle, the color yellow, the digestive system, the planet Saturn, the sweet flavor, the grains millet and barley, and the sound of singing. The "spirit" of the Spleen is "Yi,"our faculty of thought.

During late summer, Earth's nourishment is transformed into the elements of Metal, symbolized by nutrient-rich soil and rock being condensed into mineral and precious metals.

金 The METAL Phase corresponds with AUTUMN, the Lung and Large Intestine organ networks, the emotions of grief and sadness, letting go, the nose and sense of smell, inspiration, air, the skin, the respiratory system, the father, a climate of dryness, the West, harvest, the color white, the planet Venus, the pungent flavor, the rice grain, and the sound of weeping. The "spirit" of the Lung is "Po," our physical "Corporeal Soul."

Metal's descending and compressing energy begins to return nature to the depths of Water, symbolized by the dissolving of minerals and metals into ground (and ocean) water.

水 The WATER Phase corresponds with WINTER, the Kidney and Urinary Bladder organ networks, the emotion of fear, the ears and sense of hearing, darkness, mystery, the invisible and hidden, depth, death, quietude, restoration, roots, the bones, the reproductive system, the climate of cold, the North, the color black, the planet Mercury, the salty flavor, the bean legume, and the sound of groaning. The "spirit" of the Kidney is "Zhi," our Will power.

Water's deep introverted energy collects impetus (potential energy) for the new rising growth (kinetic energy) of Wood, symbolized by sap rising from the roots into the trunk, body, and branches of a tree and the emergence and rising of vital energy in our own bodies.

木 The WOOD Phase corresponds with SPRING, the Liver and Gallbladder organ networks, the emotion of anger, the eyes and sense of sight and vision, assertiveness, flexibility, creativity, new growth and beginnings, the sinews and tendons, the nervous system, a climate of wind, the East, the color green, the planet Jupiter, the sour flavor, the wheat or oat grain, and the sound of shouting or sighing. The "spirit" of the Liver is "Hun," our heavenly "Ethereal Soul."

Wood's growth provides fuel for the Fire Phase, symbolized by wood used as kindling for fire to burn, as the cycle continues into summer.

Poetry~Art

───────── ♉ ─────────

These reproductions of all-original, unmanipulated calligraphy works are available as limited series originals, prints, and greeting cards. Additional images can be viewed at the author's website: poetichealing.com

I. Catch Fire

(Fire Phase)

Black, white, and red brush and pen calligraphy on recycled cardstock with cut-outs. 27"x20.5" framed, page 4

II. Nature of the Heart

(Earth Phase)

Black brush and pen calligraphy on hand-made Mulberry paper with attached wheat stalks. 41.5"x33.5" framed, page 23

III. Alchemy

(Metal Phase)

Black brush and gold pen calligraphy, acrylic paint, on recycled cardstock with cut-outs. 27"x20.5" framed, page 44

IV. Waterboat *(excerpt)*

(Water Phase)

Black brush and gold pen calligraphy on recycled cardstock with cut-outs. 27"x20.5" framed, page 68

V. Prayer Seed

(Wood Phase)

Black brush calligraphy, acrylic paint, and fine pen on recycled cardstock with cut-outs. 27"x20.5" framed, page 81

CATCHFIRE

Walking out to sea
The body alive in purple waters
Reflecting red and orange sunrise.

What you do and live must catch
Fire to the waking depths inside you.
Do not settle for the concept of experience,
Writing what you will not lead
Or the burden of reading
What you will not be.

Following the birds to the horizon
I post this song to
Fly~

NATURE OF THE HEART

What were the body and the body of the Earth
But a brightening sky and painted ground
And an open heart such art well lived
With thoughts homeward but trails of dust
Our bones entrust. For the kindest nature there persists
Of all the wild and winged things~
A meadow's blossoms bosomed high on fragranced clouds
And billowed air, a breath the flesh does breathe in turn.

There the nature of the heart does whole
All worlds that can't be told
Nor in fancy fashioned stanzas scrolled
Save with rhythm and in rhyme
A heart with heaven finds.

For what were the body but livened soil
And what were its soul but imagined flesh
What were its joys but fleeting fires on the wind
And its sorrows but in sea and sky once drowned~
Tokens from ago now ripe,
A silenced tongue now pressed to speak.

O this form does wish to yell a pure spirit's well
For what behind this rigid mask could tell
A lovely dove's winged lifting bells.

Jack R. Wu

Like vinegar of
Expectant grapes
The heart draws inward
To the quiet chambers
Of restoration
Waiting in darkness
For resurrection
By the thirst of its own juices
Spilled by life's sacred accident
Aching with a now growing
Hopefulness that comes
With enduring grief's deliverance
From bitter days, waiting to ripen
Elegantly sour
Painfully sweet
And wisely aged
Strangely blessed, ready again
To taste the world anew.

3/14/97

"ALCHEMY"

WATERBOAT

There was only one wave that Rose from the beginning of time as a ripple in your eye, more like a rising crest of hope in the sea of your longing. So time to jump in to your boat made of water itself and learn to trust this sea loves you already, holds you and wants you to be all that it is. But your droplet must get wet with its desire for you. Let go of "I" and all you think you are here for Love requires surrender. Give your life to the ocean, to the self where there is no filling to be done, you are filled in that one act of giving up. We were all meant to swim and be swim with, not collect water into leaky vessels of thought for fear of not having enough to swim in. Your body is this current of life force waiting to join the sea. Find where the island disappears and you become the immense beauty of the world entered into its domain, its memory, its reality of the way it all began and has always been when you were too busy trying to figure out what to do with it.

Prayer seed
I release you down
Between encrusted thoughts
And rocky habits of aged terrain
To find your way into the dark
Earth of my dreams and sink
Your roots into the deep soft glow
Water of truth you find there
To drink in a vision for
Us to grow up through the center
Of my body gathering
All its cells into the clear
Green strength of your life
For us to open our leaves
To a future
Sky.

~Jack K. W.~